W9-BRR-099

Legs & Feet

Julie Murray

Peachtree

Abdo
YOUR BODY
Kids

abdopublishing.com

Published by Abdo Kids, a division of ABDO, PO Box 398166, Minneapolis, Minnesota 55439.
Copyright © 2016 by Abdo Consulting Group, Inc. International copyrights reserved in all countries.
No part of this book may be reproduced in any form without written permission from the publisher.

Printed in the United States of America, North Mankato, Minnesota.

102015

012016

THIS BOOK CONTAINS
RECYCLED MATERIALS

Photo Credits: iStock, Shutterstock

Production Contributors: Teddy Borth, Jennie Forsberg, Grace Hansen

Design Contributors: Candice Keimig, Dorothy Toth

Library of Congress Control Number: 2015941991

Cataloging-in-Publication Data

Murray, Julie.

 Legs & feet / Julie Murray.

  p. cm. -- (Your body)

ISBN 978-1-68080-159-0 (lib. bdg.)

Includes index.

1. Leg--Juvenile literature. 2. Foot--Juvenile literature.   I. Title.

612.98--dc23

                    2015941991

Table of Contents

Legs and Feet

Legs are part of your body.

You have two legs.

You use your legs to walk
and run. Ana can run fast!

You jump with your legs.

Sara jumps high!

8

Legs **bend** at the knees.

Owen bends his knee.

Feet are part of your body.

You have two feet.

Your feet help you balance.

Sam stands on one foot!

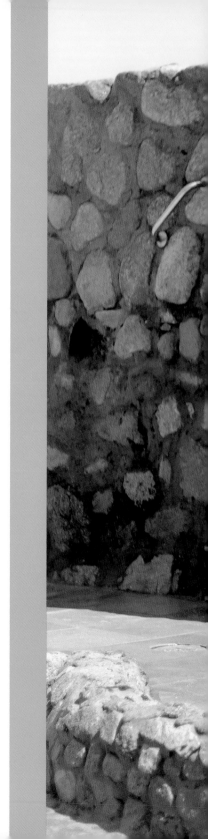

14

Each foot has five toes.

You have ten toes!

16

Ankles **connect** your feet to your legs. Your legs and feet work together.

Some animals have legs and feet. A giraffe has long legs! A kangaroo has big feet!

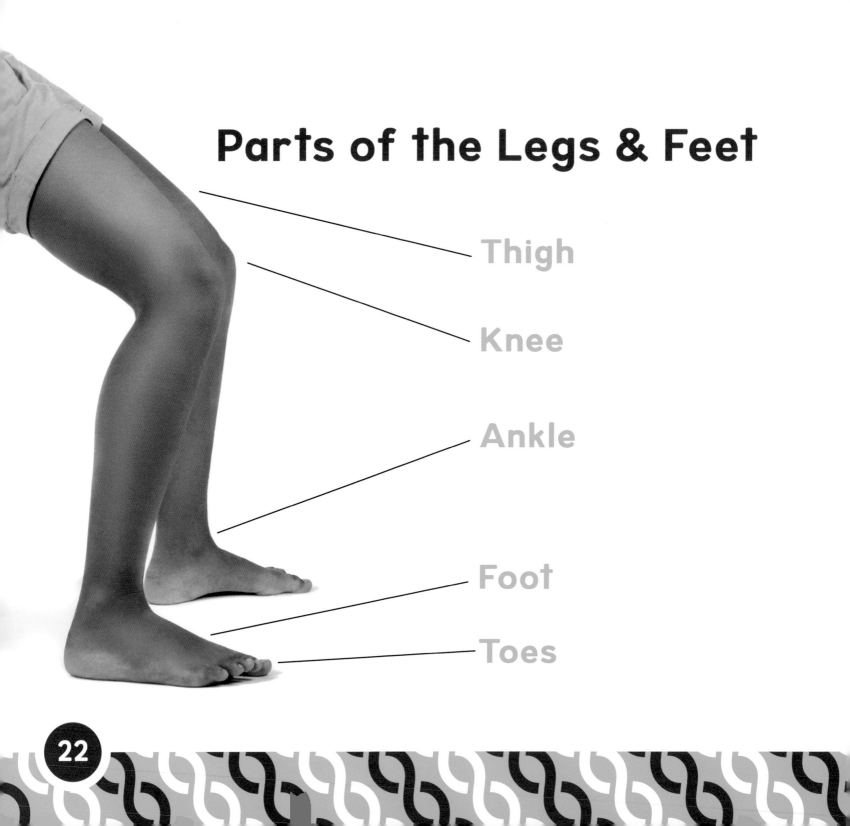

Parts of the Legs & Feet

Thigh

Knee

Ankle

Foot

Toes

Glossary

bend
move from straight to angled.

balance
even out weight to allow one
to stay upright.

connect
join two things together.

Index

abdokids.com

Use this code to log on to abdokids.com and access crafts, games, videos, and more!

Abdo Kids Code:
YLK1590